FIRESIDE

DRESSING THIN

How to Look Ten, Twenty, Up to Thirty-five Pounds Thinner Without Losing an Ounce!

by
Dale Goday

with
Molly Cochran

Design & Illustration by
Bobbi Bongard

A Fireside Book
Published by
Simon and Schuster • New York

Copyright © 1979, 1980 by Symphony Press, Inc.

Manufactured in the United States of America

An earlier edition of the work was published by Symphony Press.

TABLE OF CONTENTS

INTRODUCTION

You Can Look Thinner
Without Dieting...
Instantly!

It's true. You don't have to lose an ounce. And it doesn't matter what kind of figure you have. You can look significantly thinner, literally overnight, by introducing the techniques of DRESSING THIN into your life.

DRESSING THIN works for everybody. All you need are many of the clothes already in your wardrobe, a few odds and ends, and a thorough knowledge of how to use these things to look beautiful regardless of your weight or size. Everything you'll need to know is explained in these pages.

Here are just a few of the skinny-making tricks you'll learn about in DRESSING THIN:

—The all-important slimming line that can be incorporated into any outfit to make you look pounds thinner.

—The one ultra-comfortable garment that will make you look slim and chic, no matter what your age, shape or size.

—The two common styles which overweight women consistently wear (thinking they are slimming), which spell disaster for your looks.

—The slimming magic of scarves and beads and how to use them to your advantage.

—The thin way to stand, sit and move.

—The makeup tricks that will pare your face to proportions as slim as you want.

—The right kind of heel to make your legs look taller and slimmer immediately.

These dressing tricks, and hundreds more, will help you create a new you—a you that's slender, confident, and fashionable.

And if you *are* dieting, DRESSING THIN can make you look as though you've lost a lot more weight than you actually have—a real morale booster to make you feel that you're really getting somewhere and keep you on your diet.

Sure, we all want to look slimmer. But do we succeed? Or do we unconsciously add to our weight every time we get dressed?

The sad truth is that *most women dress fat.* You see them every day, all around you, looking as though they've all but lost control over their burgeoning bodies. And the ironic thing is that most of these women aren't really fat at all. They just *appear* heavy because of the way they dress!

You may even be one of them. Chances are good that your so-called weight problem is more in your closet than on your hips! Take a good look at your "extra" pounds, your "problem" areas. Are you working with them to make them less noticeable through clothing? Or do you somehow manage to look heavier in your clothes than out of them?

If you're like the majority of women, you're unwittingly building your whole body image around your weight, when it could well be that the way you're dressing is making you look fatter than you really are.

Try this test to find if you're one of the millions of women who are sabotaging their own cause by dressing fat:

☐ Do you sometimes buy garments which are a little snug, thinking they're incentives to lose weight?

☐ In order to get one part of a garment to fit (bust, waist, hips), do you have to buy a size that's too big for the rest of you?

☐ Do you stick to dark-colored, unobtrusive clothes that you hope no one will notice you in?

☐ Do you hardly ever get really dressed up, except on very special occasions?

☐ Do you dream of being thin and put off buying any new clothes until that glorious day when you are?

If you checked one or more items, you're dressing fat! The signal you're sending out to the world is: "I'm ashamed of the way I look. I deceive myself about my appearance. I pretend not to care. It's pointless to waste my time on me. I'm not worth it."

Pretty strong words, but we've all said them to ourselves. Our society has made us believe that Big is not Beautiful, and has given all of us who are over size 12 an inferiority complex because we don't measure up (down, rather) to the Thin Standard.

According to everything we read, hear and see, skinniness is next to Godliness. Diet your troubles away! Melt off pounds and discover happiness! Since the 1920's, the fashion industry has beaten us over the heads with its dedication to emaciation. And it's gotten worse in the past 20 years, to the point where stick-thin movie stars who live on half a grapefruit and three carrot sticks a day are offered to us in newspaper beauty columns as an ideal to aim for.

But wait just a minute! Is being cadaverous really so terrific? Is torturing your body till you could pass unnoticed through a men's locker room actually the way to beauty and pleasure?

The truth is that thin has not always been In. Look at the paintings of Reubens and Titian. Check out some pictures of the great beauties of pre-World War I days. See any hipbones on Lillian Russell? You bet your hot fudge sundae you don't. Women looked like women back then—warm, soft, fleshy, sexy. Some of us still look that way—but where are they? In the health spa, sweating away their flesh on the stationary bicycle. Or hiding out at home, fighting a losing battle with Sara Lee. Feeling ashamed of themselves for looking like women.

Big does *not* mean unattractive, and never did. But women have been deceived, intimidated and suckered mercilessly into believing that the only acceptable silhouette is that of a ruler.

LILLIAN
RUSSELL

Big does not mean unattractive, and never did.

Forget fashion designers. Forget department store PR men. Forget all the folks who make fortunes on the "thin is in" swindle. Listen to normal, healthy, sexual men. Do they like going out with what looks like a 14-year-old boy? Do they enjoy having dinner with a lady who orders unbuttered asparagus and black coffee? Is their idea of sexual bliss making love to a creaking pile of bones that threatens to pulverize on contact?

11

No.

But there's a catch. (Isn't there always?)

Look at that picture of Lillian Russell again, then look at a picture of yourself. What's the difference? How come she was the great beauty of the era, and your picture looks like Ma Kettle?

The difference is this: Lillian didn't have a weight "problem." She just had weight. She knew how to be big *and* beautiful. *Her* signal to the world was loud and clear: "I am a beauty. I dress like one, I move like one, I feel like one. Everything about me is beautiful. Men adore me, and why not? They care about me because I care about myself. You can see that just by looking at me."

Now that's the attitude to have. And that's the attitude you *will* have by the time you finish reading this book.

The point of DRESSING THIN isn't to make 200 pounds look like 100. Nobody can do that. But DRESS-ING THIN *can* make you look significantly slimmer. It can keep you, no matter what your size or shape, from looking fat. It can change your image from "that nice, chubby woman" to "that attractive, sexy, self-confident woman."

DRESSING THIN means looking good. It includes everything about how you present yourself to the world—how you dress, move and feel. It means chang-ing your life to that of a beautiful, desirable woman.

Sound like magic? It isn't. What DRESSING THIN does is offer you hundreds of carefully-researched optical illusions that you can create with clothes, accessories and makeup, plus some hardnosed advice on how to carry off these illusions to make yourself look good—not just passable, but *really* good.

So get ready for a major change in your life. From now on, you're going to be DRESSING THIN. Beginning today, you're going to be looking *good*.

1

THE THREE ESSENTIALS: COMFORT, TASTE, FIT

Comfort, taste and fit—they go hand in hand, and nothing is as important to dressing thin as these three items.

If a garment isn't comfortable, you won't enjoy wearing it, and you won't *look* comfortable. It has to suit your own personal taste, or you'll feel like you're wearing someone else's clothes. And if it doesn't fit perfectly, you'll *look* like you're wearing someone else's clothes.

Comfort: First, Last, Always

Uncomfortable clothes are fatmakers. Just as there's nothing like a pinched nerve or an aching back to make you totally miserable and unattractive, there's nothing like a tight, constricting garment—or, conversely, one that swims on you and keeps threatening to fall off—to make you look and feel dowdy, frumpy and *fat.* Uncomfortable clothes inhibit movement, too. You can't relax in them. Either you've got to hold your breath and be careful how you move lest you burst through your seams, or you've got to clutch your clothes to you to keep them from sliding away. Either way, the effect leaves an awful lot to be desired.

The woman who allows herself to be pinched, squeezed, chafed, stabbed, and otherwise tortured by her clothes simply can't look good in them, no matter how expensive they are or how much time she's spent on putting together an outfit she thinks is attractive. Whether it's a tight seam, an abrasive fabric, incorrectly-placed waistband, too-short sleeve, or clingy lining, discomfort is the first roadblock on the path toward looking good.

The problem is that most women don't realize that they don't *have* to be uncomfortable in their clothes. They were brought up to believe that "you have to suffer to be beautiful." Maybe that was true in the days when women had to crush their rib cages into tightly-laced corsets to achieve an 18-inch waistline, but it certainly isn't true today. Fortunately, we live in an age when it's not only possible, but easy to look good and feel good at the same time. All the time.

Why do so many women skulk around the house in shapeless sweatshirts and ten-year-old stretch pants, looking like over-the-hill prizefighters? Because chances are, these ghastly outfits are the only comfortable clothes they own. And anyway, they say, who cares how they look when they're vacuuming and taking out the garbage? Who's going to see them, anyway?

The mailman, for one. The Fuller Brush man. The Avon lady. The newspaper boy. And one person who can make or break your good looks by her attitude: You. Every time you pass a reflecting surface, every time you look down at your body, you see how you look— and looking sloppy isn't going to make you feel good about yourself. Looking bad says you don't think of yourself as a slim, beautifully-put-together woman. That sort of self-defeating negative attitude will do you in faster than a ten-pound box of chocolates.

Of course, looking good while you're cleaning the oven *does* present a problem. It's easy to fall into the trap of using the excuse that you're doing hard work and getting dirty anyway, and you don't want to wreck your "real" clothes. And after a while you get to think that being comfortable and looking terrible go together.

But let's face it—no big woman has any business in a sweatshirt—ever. Suppose the doorbell rings while you're in there de-greasing the oven, and your high school boyfriend, whom you haven't seen in twenty years, is standing there? And even if that doesn't happen, you've got to always look good to *you* or you won't have that positive self-image that lets you look good to everybody else.

How often have you heard someone say about a sloppy-looking woman, "She's let herself go?" She hasn't really let anything go. She just never got it together in the first place! The woman who "lets herself go" to be comfortable is making a totally unnecessary sacrifice.

I'm going to show you how to look good, not just at special times, but at *all* times, without giving up one iota of comfort. You're going to make every single garment you own a comfortable and good-looking one.

Begin by deciding which items in your closet you really *want* to own in the first place. Toss out all those nobody-will-see-me-anyway uglies—*all* of them, even your favorite schlump pants and your husband's 15-year-old madras shirt held together by two safety pins. Don't throw away your ugly "good clothes" at this point. We'll get to them later. Now make a solemn promise to yourself: "I will never look ugly again, anywhere, at any time, no matter what I'm doing."

Stick to that promise. It's the fundamental component of the new, beautiful you.

Okay, you're going to need *one* new thing right now. For housecleaning, gardening, dogwalking, errand-running, etc., invest in a pair of jeans. Yes, *jeans.* Blue jeans are America's number one contribution to international fashion, and for good reason. There's a pair for everyone, regardless of shape, size or age. Even if you've never worn a pair in your life, you'll be amazed at what they can do for you.

But be careful. No $5 flimsy second-rate jeans for you. On a big body, they'll *look* second-rate. Buy a good quality pair from a reliable maker. And this is very important: *don't buy a man's size.* The men's or "unisex" jeans are made for masculine bodies—straight up-and-down. If the hips fit you, the waist will swim; if the waist fits, you'll split the hip seams. Nowadays, top-quality jeans are made in women's sizes. Be sure to get a pair that fits you *exactly* but is a trifle long, and don't hem them until they've been washed and dried. To avoid shrinkage, take them out of the dryer while they're still slightly damp, and wear them for a while. That way, they'll fit perfectly when dry. You'll come to love them, and you'll realize that one pair of attractive, fitted jeans will perform better and be more comfortable—and *much* nicer to look at—than the six ugly knockaround outfits you've dropped into the Salvation Army box.

DRESSING
THIN

DRESSING
FAT

Be sure to get a pair of jeans that fits you properly. Gloria Vanderbilt now offers her fashionable dress jeans in woman's sizes.

Incidentally, *New York* Magazine recently tested many brands of jeans and came up with the "top ten" for fit, styling and construction. Here's their list, in descending order: Gloria Vanderbilt, Adolfo, Ralph Lauren, Calvin Klein, Liz Claiborne, Pierre Cardin, Charlotte

Ford, Studio 54, Cathy Hardwick for Best Manufacturing, and Cacharel. The all-around best is Gloria Vanderbilt—"an excellent cut, with no gapping or puckering. The waistband hugs the small of the back, as it is supposed to." The styling is subtly sexy and the construction beyond reproach. In addition, Vanderbilt has started making jeans in a new size range—women's size. That means that big women can now get the small woman's fit. Adolfo, the second best, is great too, except that the fit is "tight and European." The third, Ralph Lauren, has one fault—the waist is a little too high. The fourth and fifth, Calvin Klein and Liz Claiborne, have "good, not great" fit and some puckering at the waistband and zipper. The styling of these two is more conservative, "middle-of-the-road." The remaining five jeans all have problems with fit, (particularly at the waistline), which puckers, gaps or is too high. They are all well constructed, and while *New York* doesn't like the styling of some of them, you might want to try some or all of them and see what *you* like. If you don't exactly have an hourglass figure, the jeans with larger waists might be just right for you. Watch out for those puckered fly fronts, though —they can make your tummy look bulgy. Neat vertical stitching is a detail to aim for.

Remember that you don't *have* to wear only blue denim jeans. Most manufacturers today make jeans in a variety of fabrics and colors. Denim tends to be a slenderizing fabric because it's sturdy and holds its shape with just the right amount of give—but experiment with other colors. Khaki, for instance, is as basic and neutral as indigo blue. Other good jeans colors for big women are plum, brown, hunter green, wine, gray. Levi's now makes jeans in a sturdy, stretchy polyester in a variety of colors, but synthetics are never as comfortable as cotton, and since they don't absorb perspiration, you can't be really active in them.

So much for your basic ultra-casual garment. Now for the rest of your clothes. Divide your closet into "comfortable," "uncomfortable" and "inbetween." Take a good look at the really uncomfortable ones. How often do you wear them? And how do you feel in them?

Right. Into the Salvation Army box. Now what about the inbetweens, the ones that aren't really comfortable, but aren't excruciating either? They're salvageable. Hang onto them.

What you've got left is the core of your wardrobe. In the following chapters, we'll be pruning it some more, adding something here and there, and shaping it up so that your entire wardrobe is totally functional and each item in it makes you *look good.*

Taste: Do It Your Way

Long skirts have been fashionable for the past few years—mid-calf or even longer. But how many women really look good in them? How many looked good or even passable in the miniskirts of the 60's, or the huge crinolined and petticoated ones of the 50's? Or in fashion's latest outrage, the above-the-ankle slacks, so diabolically unattractive that they must have been designed by a man whose wife had just left him? Too many women slavishly follow fashion's dictates, no matter what these horrors make them look like.

Good taste is a matter of personal judgment, not of what haute couture designers tell us we *must* wear this season. Rule Number One is: Don't do anything

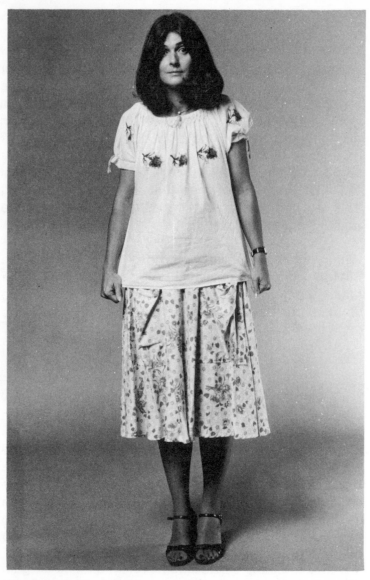

If the "peasant" look makes you look like a real *peasant, turn up your nose at it.*

you don't want to do! If you hate straight or tapered slacks, stick with flares. If the "peasant" look makes you look like a *real* peasant, turn up your nose at it. Your goal in life isn't to please some European designer whose models are all in the last stages of anorexia nervosa, but to please yourself and those around you. Be careful, though. Be sure you can tell the difference between what you really *like* and what you've just gotten used to. The long skirt is a good example. Most of us think we *ought* to like it because it's what is currently "in," and we try desperately to convince ourselves that we do, even though somewhere in the back of our minds there's that sneaking suspicion that it looks dowdy and awkward. If you have that sneaking suspicion, trust it! Wear the graceful, comfortable, not-too-short, not-too-long length that you really feel *right* in.

Good taste is a matter of quality, too—not because the amount of money you spend on a garment is important in itself, but because well-made clothes look better and last longer. A cheaply-made blouse may have insufficient seam allowances, so that the seams split easily and you let it all hang out without meaning to. There may not be enough "yoking" on a yoked back, so that the material pulls horizontally and you just look broad instead of draped. A cheaply-made skirt or pair of pants can lose its shape before the first washing. Sizes tend to run small in cheap clothes, so that to get something that's big enough in the waist, or the shoulders for instance, you have to get a size larger than you normally do—which will be *too* big somewhere else. Cheap shoes, too, are a bad bargain. Big women put a lot of strain on their feet, so good shoes pay off in the long run, in comfort and looks.

Wear the graceful, comfortable, not-too-short, not-too-long length that you feel right *in.*

Remember, a well-known label doesn't necessarily mean quality. You must check every garment yourself.

Make It Fit...Perfectly

"Fit" is an absolute word, like "pregnant." You can't be

sort of pregnant, nor can your clothes sort of fit. In order to fit at all, a garment has to fit perfectly. Otherwise, it's unusable. And it's far, far better to own a few perfectly fitting garments than three closets full of unwearable ones. With a little imagination, the few great clothes you've got left since your wardrobe purge can become dozens of slimming, dynamite-looking outfits.

Incidentally, one way to assure perfect fit is to learn to sew. Making your own means you can have all the custom-made clothes you want—including the newest styles that aren't always sold in big sizes—at tremendous savings, and a good sewing course can teach you more about clothing and proper fit than a hundred magazines. There are special "Pounds Thinner" and other slimming patterns available especially for the big woman.

A "closet fatty" is anyone who thinks of herself as fat, but won't admit it. Witness the army of size 16 women out there squashed like sausages into size 12 clothes which "sort of" fit—meaning there's barely enough blood circulating in their crushed veins to sustain life. The message these women are trying to send is, "See, I wear a 12. I'm not fat!" But the one they're *actually* transmitting is, "I'm trying unsuccessfully to pass myself off as a 12 because I can't bear to admit that I'm a big woman. I hate who I am, and that's why I'm walking around in this uncomfortable disguise."

You're a big girl now—in more senses than one—so stop playing this juvenile numbers game. Decide to look chic and terrific in a 16 if you're really a 16, rather than squashed and silly in a 12.

The flip side of this closet fatty is the size 16 woman

Do you squeeze into a size 12 when you're really a 16; do you camouflage your size 16 body in a size 20?

who deliberately drapes herself in a size 20. The hoped-for message is, "Little me. My clothes just *hang* on my itsy-bitsy body." Actual message: "I am trying to camouflage what I think is a woefully unattractive body. Nobody is allowed to see the real me."

The staple of the closet fatty's wardrobe is the Overblouse. This is a shirt, usually with a straight hemline, long sleeves, and no darts, which closet fatties wear, unbelted, over pants and skirts. The resultant line is a square, extending from shoulder to shoulder and straight down the seam. Overblouses make big women look like boxes—absolutely the worst thing possible for a big woman. There a zillion things to do with shirts to make you look slimmer, and we'll talk about them, but the Overblouse isn't one of them.

The other "camouflaging" item big women tend to wear—and ought to avoid like measles—is the Tent Dress. It makes you look like just that: a tent. Now for pregnant women the tent line is perfect: especially in a jumper, a tent-shaped garment allows room for a growing fetus and is graceful and comfortable. But for the closet fatty, who is attempting to *lie* through her clothes, the effect is quite different. The Tent shrieks: FAT!

The overblouse and the Tent are two garments that aren't really meant to fit—and don't. But what about clothes that *should* fit but don't? Here are a few simple tests you can try on your own clothes to see if they really, rather than sort of, fit:

1. Begin with undergarments. When you take off your bra and panties, are there red lines along your waist (or hips, if you wear bikinis), under your bosom, and

at the tops of your thighs? If so, your underwear is too small, and these prizewinning fatmakers are killing your looks no matter what you wear over them. They create bulges along your back, on the tummy, on the derriere, and on the legs. After all, undergarments are called "foundation" garments for a reason: they're the foundation for everything that goes on top of them. And their first requisite is that they be invisible under clothing. That means: no VPL (visible panty lines)— or other lines—and no bulges caused by too-tight underwear. Get a knowledgeable saleswoman to help you determine your correct size and style in bra, pants, girdle (if you wear one—and the right girdle can turn lumps and rolls into fluid curves) and slip. Educate yourself on the different types of bras—the plunge, décolleté, halter, strapless, "no-bra" bra, the longline, underwire, padded or softcup. Girdles and panty-

Too small undergarments create bulges along your back, on the tummy, the derriere, and the legs.

girdles range from the light-control panty all the way to the "all-in-one" corset. The bodysuit is a nifty little garment that lots of big women have discovered—it eliminates the problem of multiple underwear lines when you're wearing a sweater or slinky dress. The slacks girdle is a good idea, too—it slims you from waist to calf.

2. Look in the mirror wearing a button-front shirt or dress. If there's a gap in the button line across your bosom, one of three things is wrong: either a) the garment is too tight; b) the buttons have been positioned incorrectly; c) the straps on your bra are too loose.

You can usually correct this problem by shortening your bra straps so that a button is on the widest part of your bust. Sometimes moving the buttons over a bit will allow that needed extra bit of room. But in future, make sure the button-front garments you buy are roomy enough to avoid the fat-making bosom gap.

3. Try this simple exercise to see if your tops (including T-shirts and sweaters) are long enough: Bend to a 90° angle in front of a mirror. Does your back suddenly appear, like the snows of Kilimanjaro? The top's too short. That doesn't necessarily mean it's too small. Don't give it up if it fits through the shoulders. Just take a needle and thread, and add a cloth triangle to the back hem, with the pointy end down. That way, when you sit, you'll be sitting on the triangle, and your weight will hold the top in place.

To check for an accurate waistband, place your two thumbs inside the waistband of a skirt when you're wearing it. The thumbs should be able to slip in easily. Now hold in your stomach as much as you can and pinch the waistband together. You should not have less than one inch of fabric, and not more than two inches, in the "pinch." To check the waistband on a dress, find the narrowest part of your torso with your fingers. The waistband should be right there.

After these tests, maybe you'll find that you have to pare down your usable wardrobe a bit more. Now let's take what you've got left and see what we can do with them to make you slimmer-looking than you ever imagined possible.

2

THE THIN LINES: STYLE & DETAIL

The "Thin Lines" are the styles and details that pare inches and pounds from your looks—such things as thinning necklines, slimming sleeves, whittling waistbands. With your very first application of these principles, you'll experience a joyful change in your appearance.

The All-Important Vertical Line

The vertical line is the basis of all the thin lines. Every single optical illusion created by clothing to give the illusion of slenderness is designed to achieve the vertical line. The reason is that height is thinning, and *all thin lines are up-and-down lines.*

Just about everyone knows that a vertically-striped shirtdress creates a slimmer line than a horizontally striped one, and that thin stripes are more effective than wide stripes. But take that vertically striped dress and put over it a vest with a V-neck and points at the waist, and Voila! You've got an even slimmer line! No magic—just a vertical illusion, created by placing verticals on verticals. The combination of two V-necks (the shirtwaist collar and the vest) with the waist points on the vest and the stripes of the dress fabric pull the outfit into alignment and the effect is extremely slimming.

A vertically striped shirtdress creates a slimmer line than a horizontally striped one. Thin stripes are more effective than wide stripes.

Let's explore the areas where vertical lines are built into basic garment designs:

The neckline is probably the area with the most possibilities for dressing thin. First of all, the neckline draws attention away from other areas and toward your face, where you want it. Second, the broad horizontal expanse across the upper chest is an ideal area to establish vertical lines through clothing, accessories and jewelry. Here are some effective ways to make ordinary necklines into Thin Lines:

V-necks are just about the best Thin Line for any type of figure, because it's so versatile: it can be short or deep, casual, businesslike or dressy, plain or collared. For a collar, it can sport anything from a waist-deep shawl to an open man-tailored or button-down collar, and everything in between. It's adaptable to any style, garment, body or occasion.

V-necks can be very slimming. From left to right: a deep V creates a better vertical line than a short V; a small ruffle is okay, avoid a large one; create a deep V-neck by unbuttoning the first few buttons of a man-tailored shirt; the shawl collar can be the best slimmer, if it's deep.

For the thinnest line, keep the V-neck narrow. One of the best V-neck lines in women's dresses is the classic shawl-collared wraparound, or "bathrobe" dress, patterned after the timeless kimono-style dressing robe, which opens in front, wraps around, and ties with a

V-necks will create a flattering Thin Line for any type of figure.

self-belt. The variation with the shawl collar extending to the waist creates the most dramatically slimming vertical line of all. And when there's a self-tie belt, the ends of the belt hanging down create two additional vertical lines.

The shawl collar is a classic, and has always been fashionable; but its radically slimming look has so enchanted women that it can now be found in sweaters, blazers, two-piece knits, and blouses. Any big woman can do herself a huge favor by adding some wraparound, shawl-collared items to her wardrobe.

There's one type of V-neck the big woman should avoid, and that's the one with the huge ruffles outlining the V. A tiny ruffle is okay, provided the rest of the dress or outfit is simple; but a big ruffle will draw attention to a too-broad chest or overly-large bust.

Round necklines can be dangerous to your looks. A "jewel-neck" that lies right at the base of the neck can actually accent a pudgy neck, and is too close to a horizontal line for comfort. If you like round necklines, make sure they're deep enough so they're more elliptical or oval than round. A perfectly rounded neckline can emphasize other Rounds you'd rather not have emphasized, such as a chubby face, too-round tummy or hips. To "lengthen" the look of a rounded neckline, wear some long skinny beads or a scarf tied loosely with its ends hanging gracefully down the front (make sure it's of a fabric that drapes nicely, like silk).

The **square neckline** can be worn to advantage by big women. It's severe but elegant, and shouldn't be broken up with a scarf or beads or anything else that

A round neckline at the base of the neck looks too much like a hori-zontal line to be truly slimming.

The square neckline shouldn't be broken up by beads. For a dressy garment, keep the neckline low. Put a square-necked jumper over a turtleneck for a crisp, sporty look.

detracts from its unique beauty. If the garment's dressy, keep the neckline low, and accent it with a big pin near one of the corners. Or put a square-necked jumper over a turtleneck or cowlneck of contrasting or blending color, for a crisp, sporty look with a touch of sophistication.

Tailored collars come in several variations: Peter Pan, wing collars, and button-downs are a few of them. You can use ribbon, scarves, or fabric matching the garment to create vertical lines with one of these collars. Leaving the shirt unbuttoned to the second or third button, with an ascot, dickey or turtleneck underneath (or with just you underneath, if you're in the mood to let a little flesh show), creates a deeper V. Under a round Peter Pan collar you can tie a thin ribbon in a crisp bow; make sure it's long enough for the ends to hang more than halfway down your chest. We'll talk more about the magic of scarves and such in the chapter on accessories; but for the moment, try this: open the first two buttons of a shirt with a man-tailored collar, and put a medium-sized square scarf tied into an ascot around your neck, inside the collar. Lift the *back* of the collar so that it stands up and

37

You can use ribbons or scarves to create vertical lines with tailored collars.

gives you height. Now add a longish string of small beads. What you end up with is height at the collar, points on the collar, a deep V-neck, color near the face, and the thin line of the beads to break up the expanse of shirt fabric on the chest. This is a stylish,

The collarless shirt can be worn successfully if you remember to leave it unbuttoned at least to the second button.

feminine and Thin look which anyone can assemble to look slimmer instantly.

The collarless shirt is very fashionable right now. You can wear them successfully if you remember to leave them unbuttoned at least to the second button, to counteract the roundness of the neckline.

High necklines like **turtlenecks** can be slimming, but they need help to break the horizontal expanse across the chest. The very best way to wear a turtleneck is under another garment, preferably one with a deep neckline (a deep scoop-necked sweater looks great over a turtleneck, as does a V-necked sweater). If you wear a turtleneck alone, be sure to accessorize it with long chains, beads or pendants. Turtlenecks are almost always sporty-looking, even when paired with long evening skirts (a terrific look for a big woman, by the way) and can carry the aesthetic weight of jumbo-sized jewelry—pendants, lockets, stone, clay or porcelain beads, leather, whatever.

The **cowl neck** is a new fashion classic that combines the height of the turtleneck with the vertical line (provided you drape it correctly) that is essential for the Thin Look. Large cowls look better than small ones; after you've folded it over, pull it down in front so that the base of your throat appears.

Sleeves are extremely important to dressing thin, because the shoulder line determines the girth of the upper portion of your body. For this reason, a heavily-gathered sleeve, whether short or long, is absolutely out of the question. Opt for some more flattering ones.

The best way to wear a turtleneck is under another garment.

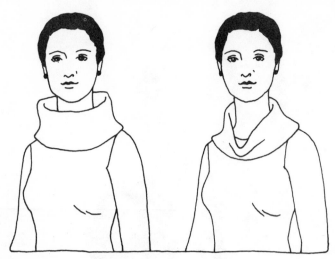

The cowl neck combines the height of the turtleneck with the vertical line, provided you drape it correctly.

Long, short, or cap, the **tailored sleeve** can't miss if the shoulder seam fits. (Avoid cap sleeves, though, if you're large-bosomed.) Remember, the line is ruined and fatmaking if the shoulder line falls off the shoulder. A rather drab-looking short tailored sleeve can be made to look more interesting if you neatly roll it up once. The soft curve it creates on your arm makes a diagonal pointing downward, rather than the horizontal line of an unrolled short sleeve. And remember that there must be plenty of room in the armhole.

The **kimono sleeve:** this straight, slightly-to-very-roomy sleeve can work wonders. For wide hips, keep the sleeve long and fairly narrow. A wide or flared kimono sleeve will give you unwanted inches at wrist—which is hip—level. For a thick waist, wear the sleeves wide and straight, and about 3/4 length. Wear with a chunky bracelet for balance. Flowing, billowing sleeves, no matter how pretty, should be reserved for evening wear.

A short tailored sleeve creates a fatmaking horizontal line. Roll it up once and you've got a soft diagonal curve pointing downward.

For wide hips, keep the kimono sleeve long and fairly narrow. A wide or flaired sleeve will give you unwanted inches at the wrist—which is hip level.

Seamed diagonally from armpit to neckline, the **raglan** "**sleeve**"—which is really just a seam line, and not a separate sleeve at all—is a terrific Thin Line. It cuts shoulder width *and* breaks the horizontal chest area. The raglan seam can carry either a plain tailored sleeve, a kimono sleeve or a dolman (batwing), which is *the* great sleeve for chubby arms. Since the drama is built into the sleeve itself, keep a dolman-sleeved garment simple. No ribbons or scarves (except perhaps a small square used as a choker—try turning it so the knot's in the back). Strong, plain jewelry only.

The raglan sleeve is a terrific *Thin Line.*

The **sleeveless** look is a great vertical line, but it's for you *only* if you have fairly slender arms. It's the kiss of death for plump upper arms. But if you've got acceptable arms and a wide chest or waist, a sleeveless garment in which the armhole is cut fairly close to the neck at top is narrowing.

44

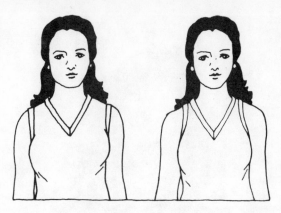

The sleeveless look is the kiss of death for plump upper arms. A sleeveless garment with the armhole cut fairly close to the neck at the top is narrowing.

Remember to avoid 3/4 length sleeves of any kind if you have particularly heavy forearms or thick wrists— these will only emphasize the lower arm and wrist area. Short sleeves, or long sleeves almost touching the hand, are for you—with wide or bulky bracelets, or several delicate or thin bracelets together. Avoid *one* thin bracelet on a heavy arm or wrist.

The Waistband. There are two main shapes in waist-bands: the straight, conventional type suitable for belting, and the curved band that fits on the hips. The straight type is the more slimming for thick middles *if it's not tight!* Don't allow yourself to be even a little bit of a closet fatty on this point! If the waistband doesn't fit your waist (relaxed) perfectly, your tummy will bulge out beneath it, saying FAT for all the world to see. Also, the straight waistband looks neater, and works better with jackets and blazers.

A variation of the straight waistband is the dropped waistline (as in the "blouson," a currently popular look).

Remember to avoid 3/4 length sleeves.

The two main shapes in waistbands: the straight and the curved.

It lengthens the waist, so it's good for short-waisted women. But don't wear it if you're very wide-hipped, unless you're also quite tall—and then, wear it in a soft, drapable fabric. Many blousons have a drawstring tie at the bottom which you can let hang down to give one of those important verticals.

The curved band is a good line for short-waisted women too, as it lengthens the waist and cuts a scoop into the derriere, reducing it phenomenally.

Stay away from wide waistbands (and wide belts) unless you're very long-waisted.

The skirt can be one of your greatest assets if you know how to choose the correct styles. Before we talk about specific styles, a word about hemlines: the fashion industry has tyrannized us for years with its up-again down-again hemline. Their motto seems to be, What goes up must come down, and vice versa. No changee-no monee for the fashion people. But *much* money out of your pocket into theirs, if you allow yourself to be a slave to designers' whims. Pick a skirt length that is most flattering to *you* and have the guts to stick with it—that's *really* being fashionable. And for most large women, the most flattering length is about one or two inches below the knee, at the slimmest part of the upper calf. A hemline that cuts lower, across the widest part of the calf, will make your calves look like tree trunks. For evening, go really long—just above the ankle or lower. The long sweep of a graceful skirt, especially one with good vertical lines, is one of the best things that can happen to you. It's instant glamour, femininity, poise and slimness. But since you'll be wearing shorter skirts most of the time, let's get back to them:

The **dirndl** or **gathered skirt** is an absolute no-no. It makes your hips and tummy look bigger; it flows out right where it should flow *down.* Darts, yes; gathers, *no.*

The **straight skirt** is another disaster for a woman who's carrying around some extra poundage. Like the overblouse, which we talked about earlier, it will make you look like a box—and there isn't much that's sexy, feminine or beautiful about boxes.

Two more "no's" and we'll get to some "yeses." The "no's" are the circle skirt—just too much width and flare for you—and the all-around pleated skirt, which lets the hips and tummy bulge out just as the gathered skirt does.

DRESSING
FAT

DRESSING
THIN

*Gathered skirts are an absolute no-no. Look for details that add
vertical lines, like a slimming front seam.*

So much for the skirts to skirt quickly by. Now for the
ones to head for: first, the *stitched-down pleated skirt.*
Pleats that are stitched down neatly over the hips and
then allowed to flow freely give you precisely what

we're looking for in a skirt: a gentle A-line (not a huge wide A, remember!). The *wrap skirt* can do the same thing; and its self-tie gives you additional vertical lines. The *darted A-line skirt* is going to be your Old Faithful, but you won't tire of the style if you look for (or add yourself, if you sew) details that make for variety: Buttons down the front. A mock-fly front. Vertical pocket flaps (not right on the hips, though). Notice that all these details are verticals.

If it's not clear already, let me add that fussy skirts are to be avoided. Don't buy a cotton skirt with a huge ruffle at the bottom, for instance. Or a corduroy with buttons, pockets and pleats. A skirt's message should be, "See how strikingly simple I am." It should never draw the attention away from what's above it, but should quietly and tastefully blend in to the total look.

Pants and **pantsuits** are still attractive, practical and popular women's garments, though studies have shown that they project somewhat less authority in the office than more traditional feminine clothing. Still, trousers can't be beat on cold winter days, and a good pantsuit in the right fabric can make you look like a million. Many of the same principles apply to pants as to skirts. No gathered tops. No knits—they bulge! (We'll talk about fabrics later.) The fit of pants is particularly important, because they're a more body-revealing garment than skirts. It's worth spending a few extra dollars to get well-made, well-fitting pants, and, if necessary, to have them altered so the fit is *perfect.* They must not be too tight at the hips and derriere—but baggy is just as bad.

To flare or not to flare? That is *the* question for pants-minded women these days. If you can manage to

No gathered tops. No knits—they bulge! Concentrate on creating the perfect optical illusion for you.

ignore fads and concentrate instead on creating the perfect optical illusion the admiring looks you'll get will reward you for your courage. In the momentous

The tight, skinny pants leg will make the hips look much wider than the legs. It's a definite Out.

question of leg width, extremes are not for you. Sailor-flares, harem pants, tapered pants, and the tight, skinny pants leg are definitely Outs. The optical illusion that says Thin is most effectively created by the moderately wide leg, straight or *gently* flared. It will keep the hips from looking much wider than the legs—which we don't want—and it will conceal any bulges or less-than-perfect contours.

As for pants length, too-short pants look plain silly, no matter what Paris fashion designers try to push on us. Full-length pants (as opposed to shorts) should *be* full length, which means covering the top of the shoe but *not* dragging on the ground. When you shop for pants, wear the shoes you'll be wearing with the pants, so you can check the length. A length that's perfect for a mid-high heel will get stepped on if you wear flats.

Tops: We talked about these in our discussion of necklines, sleeves and such; but there's a bit more to be said about them. Sweaters and blouses, like pants, should be neither tight nor baggy. They should fit gently, suggesting your curves without clinging to them.

Avoid bulky sweaters, even in the coldest weather. Instead, for warmth, try layers of lightweight sweaters —a thin turtleneck under a thin V-neck, for example. You can layer blouses with sweaters, too—try a short-sleeved, scoop-necked sweater over a long-sleeved, tailored-collar blouse. For tops, a tapered look is more feminine and flattering than a straight one; for those that are worn outside your skirt or pants, moderately long is more thinning than short. A short top puts a horizontal line right across the hips and tummy, and

Avoid bulky sweaters, even in the coldest weather.

you know how *that* looks! Oddly enough, many over-weight women have too-flat buttocks. The flesh is on the hips and tummy, rather than on the derriere itself. Semi-fitted tops that fall to the top of the thighs (just about where your panty line is on the side) actually cover up the problem. A long-ish tunic, perhaps loose-ly belted with a self-belt and not tight around the hips, is great for both tummies and hips.

Jackets are nearly always slimming. as long as they're not "boxy" or too short. They should be neat, simple and tailored—not too wide at the shoulders—and should come just about to the bottom of the buttocks. Avoid double-breasted styles, particularly if you're large-busted or wide-shouldered; and remember that a long, narrow collar is the most slenderizing. If the jacket has long vertical seams in front, bravo. Wear the jacket open, and you've got umpteen vertical lines to slim you (a tailored blouse underneath will give you even more; a turtleneck looks terrific too).

The **skirted suit,** we're told by people who should know, is the success-and-power outfit of the office these days. Good ones are expensive, so if you can afford only one, make it the best you can buy. It should be on the conservative side without being severe—no flounces or embroidery, fitting perfectly at the shoulders, waist and hips, the skirt falling just a bit below the knee. The jacket should be button-able, even if you wear it open, and the sleeve length just over the wristbone. Stick to dense, but not heavy, fabrics that hold their shape well, in natural fibers. Ever wonder why only the beefiest businessmen look fat? It's because the suit is a slimmer. Make it work for you to project the competence-cum-femininity you can carry better than any skinny!

A short top puts a horizontal line right across the hips and tummy.

A tucked-in blouse with a slimming belt makes all the difference in the world.

Avoid double-breasted styles; long, narrow collars are the most slenderizing.

Vests are plentiful in department stores, and they're easy to knit or sew. Tailored vests that button down the front, have V-necks and points at the bottom are great. If you've got a round-necked vest, wear a tailored collar with points underneath it.

Vests that button down the front and have V-necks are great.

Jumpers cut in the "princess" style are the ultimate slenderizing silhouette.

The **jumper,** however, is an unjustly neglected garment. Jumpers give variety to your wardrobe; the armholes create vertical lines; and most jumpers are cut in the "princess" style which is the ultimate slenderizing silhouette—skimming over the waist without nipping in, and then a narrow A-line to the hem.

The **dress** is still what makes a woman look like a woman—but it must be the right kind of dress. Like the jumper, the dress can give an unbroken line from neck to hem, and that's a plus for the Thin Look—but it must be the right kind of dress. Again, the princess is the line of choice; but it needn't be boring. You can achieve variety through color, fabric and pattern (which we'll get to shortly) and, of course, through detail. What you do with the dress can keep you from getting tired of it, too. A simple, well-tailored dress can be dressed up or down with jewelry, scarves, vests and jackets.

But you shouldn't feel that there's *nothing* you can wear but the princess line. A belted dress can be slimming, if the belt is a narrow one, and preferably of the same material as the dress—*and* so long as it's not too tight. A blouson-type dress, with some fullness above the waist and an A-line skirt, is graceful on a big woman. Shirtdresses are terrific, especially those that button all the way down the front. Just be sure the dress is somewhat wider at the hem than at the hips so it doesn't "box" you.

A word of caution: stay away—far, far away—from the new (old) broad-shouldered style Paris has just resurrected out of the wreckage of the 40's. Some of these styles will make you look like a Nazi general, and even the least offensive of them will make you look broad,

The dress can give an unbroken line from neck to hem, and that's a plus for the Thin Look.

62

A belted dress can be slimming, if the belt is a narrow one of the same material as the dress.

A blouson-type dress, with some fullness above the waist is graceful on a big woman.

64

top-heavy and tough. They can be summed up in one word: ugh.

If you live in an area of the country that has cold winters, your **coat** can make or break your appearance for several months in the year. After all, it's all that most people will see of your clothing (besides accessories); and if you feel tempted to say, "Who cares what all those nameless strangers think," remind yourself, quick, that that's an absolutely deadly attitude. Not because it's really crucial what *they* think, but because of what not caring does to the way *you* think of yourself. It can't be said too often: to look good, you've got to feel good about yourself, not just when you're at a party or at work or at the theater, but *all* the time— which includes when you're cleaning the oven or fighting cold and slush on city streets.

So much for the pep talk, now for the specifics. In a coat, you want to aim for maximum warmth with minimum bulk. Stay away from furs and fake furs; they'll make you look like a stuffed animal—soft, cuddly and *chubby*. But a fur or fake fur collar and cuffs is fine; it's elegant-looking, the collar draws attention to the face and it creates height. The line should be long and semi-straight, as with a dress; that is, it should nip in *slightly* in the waist area and the hem should be a bit wider than the hips. The coat can be self-belted or not, but stay away from the ones with very wide belts. Go with classic, tailored styles, avoid gimmicks, gadgets and fussiness.

In raincoats, check for durability and water repellence first. Seek out a strong but soft fabric that drapes well —no cardboard coats, and no silk, which loses its shape too easily. The classic trenchcoat looks good

Stay away from furs and fake furs; they'll make you look soft, cuddly and chubby.

The classic trenchcoat looks good on almost everyone, but keep in mind there's a tremendous variety of slimming rain fashions.

on almost everyone, but there's tremendous variety in rain fashions. The shiny, wet-look raincoats hang beautifully, but their rubber-on-canvas counterparts are notorious fatmakers. Stick to full-length coats or capes rather than ponchos: anything shapeless is a no-no.

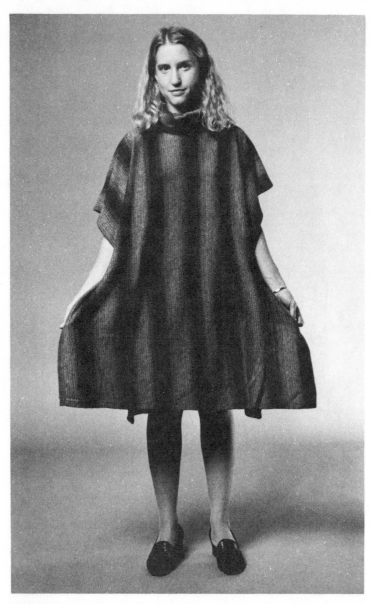

Stick to full-length coats or capes rather than ponchos: anything shapeless is a no-no.

Now that you know everything you always wanted to know (but didn't know whom to ask) about your most flattering and slimifying lines in all sorts of garments, you're almost ready to send the new you out to take the world by storm. But not quite. We still have to talk about some awfully important elements of your looks: pattern, color and fabric. Any one of them, wrongly chosen, can ruin the most brilliantly put-together outfit and sabotage all your efforts at slenderness.

3

PATTERN, COLOR, FABRIC

Color

Remember the Ann Sothern Show during the good old days of black and white TV? Ann was a study in the slimming magic of contrasting colors, with only black and white to work with. All of her outfits on the show were black and white so that nothing she wore appeared gray; and all of them reflected consummate care in designing Thin Lines. So great was the thinning power of those garments that you may not even have noticed that Ms. Sothern is far from skinny. On the contrary, she's a wonderful example for all of us to follow: beautiful, vivacious, charming *and* abounding in feminine flesh.

Disregard everything you've read about how big women have to stick to dark colors. Untrue! Nothing's as depressing as seeing a woman hide herself in blacks, browns and navy blues day after day. However, as with everything, alas, there's a caution here. Wearing a light, bright color on a particular problem *area* will draw attention to that area—and that problem. In other words, if you're particularly wide-hipped, you won't want to wear a light-colored skirt or pants with a dark top and shoes. If you're a bit top-heavy, a light top with a dark skirt or pants will emphasize it. However,

If you're wide-hipped, you won't *want to wear a light-colored skirt with a dark top.*

you *can* wear a light colored dress, suit or coat, or an outfit in coordinated light colors, because that's a total, balanced look: it won't make a particularly cumbersome part of you seem out of proportion. And provided you choose your lines, colors, patterns and fabrics carefully, according to the guidelines in this book,

If you're a bit top-heavy, a light top with a dark skirt will emphasize it.

there's no reason why you can't wear white, or pale green, or whatever light, gay color suits your fancy— and your own coloring.

The slenderizing secret of color is *contrast*—and it's a lot more subtle than a simple light-top-dark-bottom combination. Wear a green button-front shirt with a white collar and cuffs, or a white shirt with plaid collar and cuffs—they'll give you height, neckline interest, and pizzazz. Wear a white shirtwaist with *black* front buttons and a thin black belt; unbutton the top button; add a short, jaunty scarf at the neck and a black cardigan, and you've assembled a thinning, interesting outfit. Try a plain white shirt with a peter pan collar and tie *two* long, skinny red ribbons in a bow under neckline. Take the plainest solid-color A-line dress you've got and put a tweedy blazer over it. Now take a long, printed scarf and wrap it around your neck like a soft turtleneck, and you're ready to take on the supermarket or the office!

Contrasting colors break up horizontal lines, thereby creating vertical lines. To make color work best for you, try to keep your dark colors to the *outside* of your ensemble, building up bright or light colors toward the center. This is done easily through the use of dark-colored blazers and sweaters. The dark-on-the-outside plan is simply a rule of thumb, however. White sweaters are pretty. Just avoid wearing them with white shirts. Instead, contrast them with a dark or bright solid, either underneath or on top. And a beige, tan or light grey coat can be very slimming if it has a darker lining and collar (especially a shawl collar!).

Consider your own hair and skin tones when you're choosing colors. In general, dark women can wear bright colors wonderfully and look terrific in pastels too; the only colors they should avoid are the really drab ones—dull brown, khaki, charcoal gray—unless these are given a lift by contrasting brights. Blondes, too, look marvelous in just about any color (except, perhaps, yellow); but those with skin tones that tend more towards the yellow than the pink should avoid

The slenderizing secret of color is contrast. *A white shirt with contrasting buttons and a dark or bright scarf at the neck creates vertical lines.*

To make color work best, keep dark colors to the outside of your ensemble, building up bright or light colors toward the center.

orange and orange-red shades as well as the yellow-tinted peach tones (the pink-tinted peach shades are fine). Women with in-between hair shades (light brown, dark blonde) will benefit far more from clear, bright colors than foggy or mousy ones. Redheads and the auburn-haired generally look their best in the cool shades, which includes all the browns, greens, blues, purples, greys, white—everything but yellow, orange, pink and red. But they can be guided by their skin tones: some red-haired women can be stunning in certain shades of orange and peach; and rust and terra cotta, which do include red tones, are marvelous on most redheads. Gray-haired women, like blondes, can wear pastels or brights as well. An especially flattering touch for any woman is to wear near the face (in a blouse, sweater, collar or scarf) a color which matches or intensifies the color of her eyes. If your eyes are blue-gray, wearing a clear blue will make them look bluer. If they're nondescript brown, a warm rich brown will make them look softer, more inviting. And so on.

Fabric

We're in luck! The bulky, for-skinnies-only-fabrics that flooded the fashion market for years have finally bitten the dust. The new "in" fabrics are soft, slimming and natural: silk, cotton, linen and soft wool. Also, we have a tremendous range of synthetics today, some of which are such good imitations of natural fibers that it's really hard to tell the difference.

Here's a rundown on the four basic natural fabrics:

Silk may just be the most exquisitely feminine fabric ever developed. Beautiful women have been taking advantage of its softness, its quiet, sexy rustle, its

Every beautiful woman should own at least one real silk blouse.

cool feeling and graceful, flowing charm for thousands of years. Silk *screams* money, elegance, fashion and sex. It drapes magnificently. It comes in many weaves, from the sheerest Indian silks to dense, heavy satins. You can buy pure silk in everything from T-shirts to raincoats, but it's prettiest in blouses and dresses.

Silk's drawbacks are cost, maintenance (you don't dare spill anything on it, or let it get caught in the rain) and wear expectancy (far shorter than synthetics). Also, silk feels cool on the skin, but it's a rather warm fabric to wear, like nylon. If you perspire heavily, you have to be careful.

Every beautiful woman should own at least one real silk blouse if possible. If you're going to own *one,* though, make it a heavy, matte silk—no sheers, please, and no satin. They're for skinnies only—the sheer because of its super-revealing qualities, the satin because it tends to reflect light in all the wrong places. Silk is the epitome of party looks, it's great in the office, and it's the chic-est chic with casual pants and even jeans! But if you consider it just too expensive or too delicate (and it has to be admitted that it's not the world's most practical fabric), the silk-polyester blends and polyester silk look-alikes are terrific, too. They combine the beauty and lightness of silk with wearability and practicality. They're washable, generally don't need ironing, and will last longer than silk. There are polyesters now that are woven to look like silk crepe de chine, silk georgette (a thin, nearly sheer weave), silk jersey and other luscious looks.

Cotton is practical in many ways (but not all), comfortable, adaptable to any style from shorts to evening gowns. Perspirers know that cotton is *the* fabric to

No synthetic can remain as brilliantly white as cotton.

wear in summer. Cotton is a fashion classic, and has never been more in style than right now. Its crispness seems to radiate "clean," and no synthetic can remain as brilliantly white as cotton. This year, "big-tops" in cotton and other fabrics are very fashionable; you can wear these as long as they fit in the shoulders and don't have fullness in the upper arms. Cotton is tremendously versatile. It comes in all sorts of knits and weaves; in very light to very heavy weights; it can be stiff, like cotton duck or canvas, and quite soft, like cotton knits and gauzes.

Cotton does have some drawbacks, as do all natural fibers. You have to iron it, unless it's the crinkly kind of cotton that's supposed to stay crinkly, as in Indian shirts. The alternative is to send it to a laundry with explicit instructions to put your cotton garments on hangers, but even then, commercial presses usually leave fatmaking creases. It's for this reason that cotton doesn't travel well, and your wardrobe should include cotton/polyester blends, which look great, feel *almost* as good, and are much easier to care for.

(Note: Some fabric manufacturers have come up with a permanent-press process for cotton, bless them! It's not as widely available yet as the ordinary wrinkle-prone cottons, but as the idea catches on, more and more cotton garments will be iron-free.)

Two more drawbacks: cotton tends not to hold its shape as well as synthetics. When it stretches, it stays stretched. When it's machine-washed and machine-dried, it shrinks—sometimes very badly. For this reason, too, blends are more practical. And pure cotton, alas, doesn't last as long as synthetics and blends. Cotton corduroys, for example, will wear out far more quickly than cotton-polyester corduroys. However, if super-long wear isn't a concern of yours, if you're careful about washing and drying, and if you don't mind ironing (or have someone to do it for you), cotton is cool, comfortable, classic—and classy.

Linen, unfortunately, is bad news for big women. It wrinkles practically on sight, loses its shape easily and sweating in linen—even a little bit—is *verboten.* Just sitting on linen makes dramatic creases, and as you know, creases are spelled F-A-T. It's a deliciously cool fabric, though, and looks rich, expensive and feminine. If you're a linen-lover, restrict your use of it to summer party (of the stand-up, air-conditioned variety) dresses. There's nothing keeping you from the great linen look-alike polyesters, though, complete with the little nubs that are linen's trademark. They travel like crazy, and don't leave you looking like you've slept in your clothes.

Thank the Lord for **wool**—it's almost impossible to look anything but good in wool garments that fit and are well-made. Real wool always looks like money, and it's still not terribly expensive. There are so many varieties of wool, from twill and gabardine to felt and worsted, that it would take a catalogue to list them all. This year's fashion magazines are full of yummy soft wools for fall, winter and spring, and most of them are finely-woven—good news because a fine weave means dense fabric that drapes and moves well, particularly if it's cut on the bias. You can wear wool in blouses, sweaters, skirts, pants, dresses, suits, blazers, or coats, and they'll all look great as long as you stick with finely-woven wools. Avoid bulky or stiff wools, anything resembling burlap, or any heavily-textured wool. Fishermen's sweaters are not for you; neither are fluffy angoras and mohairs.

To determine if a wool is dense enough, hold it up to artificial light. If the fabric blocks out all the light, it's right. To see if it's too stiff, hold the garment at arm's length and move it from side to side. If the wool doesn't sway and fold a little, it's probably a fatmaker.

The ideal wool for large women is gabardine. It's very dense; it hangs and moves like silk, yet it's heavy and holds its shape. It wears well. It takes color magnificently. It looks terribly expensive. It can handle a reasonable amount of perspiration. It's durable. And it lasts forever in virtually the same condition in which you bought it.

The only drawbacks to wool are that it has to be dry-cleaned and that some people are allergic to it. If wool makes you itch, try a gabardine garment with a heavy lining. Gabardine is so finely-woven that it shouldn't be irritating. But if it is, forget wool. Comfort first!

The fashion industry, which occasionally comes up with some good ideas to balance out all the frightful ones, has recently created polyester-wool blends, which look like wool, feel softer, and are often washable! You can also find wool in combination with other synthetics in sweaters, and sometimes combined with silk in fine dresses.

If we seem to have been pushing polyester, it's not because we're getting paid off by the polyester manufacturers; it's because it is generally the best of the synthetics for looks, performance and versatility. It combines beautifully with natural fabrics and all by itself it can look like silk, linen, cotton and (almost) like wool jersey. Polyester double-knits were created to be a wool look-alike, but they don't quite make it, and unfortunately, so much polyester double-knit has been bought and worn in the past ten years that it has become a fashion joke. Don't wear it.

There are other good synthetics: Orlon and Dynel are excellent acrylic fibers (but a word to the wise—be-

Avoid horizontal lines and large plaids.

ware of cheap acrylics! They'll look like shapeless rags after they've been washed once). In general, well-known brand name fabrics will perform well. Nylon and rayon have been around for a long time, and you probably are pretty familiar with what they can and can't do. Rayon is enjoying something of a comeback, particularly in combination with wool or polyester.

Pattern

You've got a large part of the pattern problem solved if you stay away from horizontal lines: that's the first axiom. The second is, avoid large plaids. After that, you're pretty much on your own. Solid colors or small, all-over patterns tend to be the most slimming, because they break up the body line least. But you can get sick of them, and nobody wants you to be bored with your clothes. So vary your wardrobe: wear vertical and diagonal stripes, narrow, wide or a mixture; small checks; any kind of print, small or large, so long as it's an all-over print and does not create horizontals (step back from it about 10 feet and narrow your eyes; the details will disappear and you'll see the basic lines of the print). Don't be afraid of dramatic, unusual patterns; the big woman can carry them off with dash and flair. Try a wrap skirt and matching shawl in a dramatic Indian print with its vivid reds, blues, greens; a dolman-sleeved dress of vertical stripes, different widths, in plum, mauve, deep purple and black; a rose tweed suit with a blouse of white daisies on rose, an A-line challis skirt with an all-over print of multicolored flowers on black (these are all clothes actually on the market). Actually, you needn't worry too much about pattern right now, because far more solids than patterns are currently being shown—solids in colors so

Don't be afraid of dramatic, unusual patterns; the big woman can carry them off with dash and flair.

luscious you'd like to eat them. But when you do wear a pattern, make it a beautiful one—and watch the heads start turning in admiration.

4

ACCESSORIES

Accessories are the frosting on the cake (which you shouldn't eat), the dressing on the salad—in short, the finishing touch, without which your outfit isn't complete and you yourself look somehow unfinished, not-quite-together. And the right accessories can do a lot to heighten the illusion of slenderness that you create with your clothes, hairstyle, makeup and bearing. Besides, knowing that your shoes, purse, jewelry, scarf, whatever are perfect gives you an extra little lift, a sense of confidence in the way you look that *has* to make you look even better than you already do (and if you've been paying attention, you're well on your way to looking absolutely splendid).

First, your **shoes.** Here, as with your clothes, comfort should be your first concern. If your shoes don't fit perfectly and feel great, they're going to hurt eventually—and there's nothing attractive or sexy about the look of agony that sore feet can cause. So steer a very wide course around cheap shoes—this is *not* a place to be budget conscious at the expense of your poor feet, which have enough problems simply doing their job (do you realize how much pressure we put on our feet in simple walking?). These days, it's unlikely you can get a well-made shoe for less than $20 to $25 unless you find a terrific sale, and you may

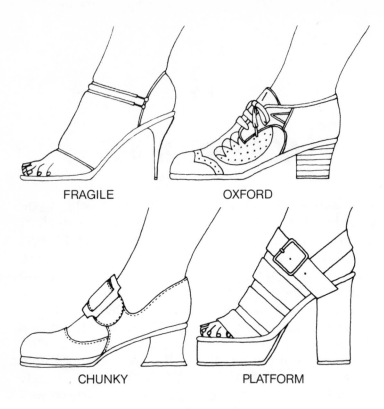

FRAGILE   OXFORD

CHUNKY   PLATFORM

Shoes to avoid

wind up spending up to $40 to $50 or even more for the perfect shoe. But it'll be worth it in terms of comfort, looks and wear—your feet and your whole appearance will thank you. Spend time having the shoes fitted. Walk around in them for a while before you buy. Wear them in your home, on carpeted floors, before you wear them out on the street, so that if there are any problems with the fit, you can take them back with no signs of having been worn.

As a general rule, look for shoes in dark, neutral colors. You don't want them to draw attention away from the

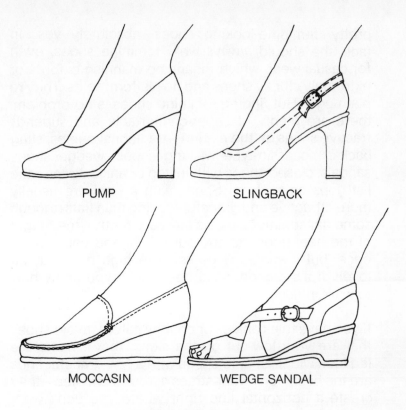

PUMP   SLINGBACK

MOCCASIN   WEDGE SANDAL

Shoes to look for

rest of you; your shoes should complement your outfit and harmonize with it; they should never dominate it. Shoes should be the same color as, as dark as, or darker than, your dress, skirt or pants, though they need not necessarily be in the same color group: you can certainly wear wine-colored shoes with a navy blue outfit, black shoes with a red outfit, brown shoes with gray clothes. But the color shouldn't clash or distract.

The big woman should stay away from extremely fragile-looking shoes. She's not the fragile type. But pretty, feminine-looking shoes—absolutely yes. In fact, she should *always* wear feminine shoes, even for casual wear, which means no mannish oxfords or extremely clunky shoes and no platform soles. They're plain ugly. But finding feminine shoes is no problem: there are plenty of super-comfortable and super-attractive shoes on the market—traditional pumps, slingbacks, mocassin-type walking shoes, wedge shoes, sandals, closed shoes with instep or ankle straps—the list goes on and on. Shoes with a heel are usually more attractive and graceful-looking than flats (though some flat summer sandals are very pretty); the height of the heel depends on your height and your preference, but it shouldn't be spiky. A high heel can be lovely if it's a good, solid heel and *if* you know how to walk in it.

If you have thick ankles or chubby calves, avoid shoes that are very low-cut on the sides; they'll make the leg look wider. Simple shoes with a few graceful lines are the best; don't wear straps across the instep—they create a horizontal line right where you don't want it; and two-tone shoes break up the line of the foot and make the leg look stubbier.

Of course, match the type of shoe you're wearing to the purpose of your outfit. You wouldn't wear an evening sandal or dressy pump with your work or sports clothes; you won't wear a moccasin with a cocktail dress. And one final note: take care of your shoes. Shoes with worn-down heels or soles, soles that are separating from the shoe, scuffs and scrapes, are not attractive—in fact, they're quite the opposite.

Boots are essential footwear in cold climates. Many of the rules for shoes apply to boots: they shouldn't

Knee-high boots will create height and flatter you more than the mid-calf length or the shorties, which create horizontals across your ankle or calf.

be mannish or clunky; they should be of a neutral color that complements your coats and blends in with all your outfits. Boots with heels (they needn't be high) are more slenderizing than flat ones; and most of the boots sold today do have at least a moderate heel.

The knee-high ones will create more height and flatter you more than the mid-calf length or the shorties, which create horizontals across your ankle or calf. Avoid the western-type boots which have a straight line from foot to knee; the contoured ones are far more feminine.

You can tuck narrow-legged pants into knee-high boots, but wear wide-leg pants outside your boots. And don't wear boots with dressy clothes—if you need protection from the weather when you're dressed to kill, take along a pair of dressy shoes in a plastic bag or in your purse.

Since nearly all women carry a **handbag** nearly all the time, it's an important part of your total look. You'll want to consider size, shape, color, material and convenience when selecting a handbag, because any one of these can affect your appearance negatively or positively.

A big woman should not carry a teeny handbag. Like the too-fragile shoes, it just looks silly, as though she's pretending to be little, helpless and oh-so-delicate. A woman who's both large and tall can—in fact, should —use a bag that's a good size, but not enormous. If you're short, your handbag should be about 8-10 inches in width (slightly smaller, if you wish, for evening).

To shoulder the bag or not? Shoulder bags are convenient—they leave both hands free. But if you have sloping shoulders, they won't work for you. Use a clutch bag, or one with a strap you sling over your arm or hold in your hand. If you use shoulder bags, make sure they don't hang right at your hip level, or they'll accentuate the hips. There are shorter ones which hang at about waist level, or a longer one may have adjustable straps. Below the hips is too long—it will flap against your body when you move, unless you hang on to it at all times—and that defeats the purpose of a shoulder bag.

As for the material of the handbag, leather is the all-time favorite. It wears best and always looks distinguished. Vinyls that look like leather are fine, too, but stay away from those that look like the plastics they are—the shiny, stiff ones. Leather has a matte, understated look, which is what gives it its elegance. Canvas is sporty, and since it's far less expensive than leather, you can have several canvas bags if you like—but don't buy the very colorful, two-or-three tone ones unless you're planning to use them at the beach or on picnics. You'll find lots of other fabrics in handbags, too—corduroy, tapestry, linen, denim; just let your good taste be your guide. Straw, of course, is for summer or warm climates; there's a delightful variety of straw and rope handbags available now; the only ones you should *never* use are the basket types—they're just too cutesy for words.

As for color, your handbag doesn't have to match your shoes, but it should harmonize with them and with your ensemble. For instance, with a pale green sweater and a green-and-brown checked skirt, you might wear dark brown shoes and a dark green corduroy bag. Or a brown handbag with a medium-blue suit, cream-colored shirt and navy shoes (brown handbags go with everything; black, once considered the neutral of neutrals, is less versatile and you'll tire of it more quickly). Try a dark red bag and shoes with a navy-and-white outfit—stunning! Or the same bag and shoes with a mauve dress—different and dramatic. Most good bags today come in sumptuous colors like burgundy, taupe, cognac, camel in addition to the usual brown, black and navy.

Stockings (which are usually pantyhose) are a real fashion accessory today, with all the colors and textures available. Darker shades create an illusion of slenderer legs than light ones (*never* wear the white-tinted stockings that were popular a few years ago!) and there are vertically-patterned weaves that add to that all-important Thin Line. Dark-tinted, vertical-patterned stockings can make heavy legs seem to lose a good inch in width. Stick to neutral shades, though, unless you want to match your stockings or pantyhose to your sweater or blouse (a fine idea, as long as the color isn't too bright and distracting, so the eye is drawn back and forth between legs and chest), or color-key them to your skirt or dress (pale gray stockings with a gray skirt; brown-tinted stockings with a brown print dress, etc.) Remember that if you're putting color on your legs, it must be done with a light touch and a sure hand. If you're not supremely confident about your taste, stick to the neutrals—you'll feel more comfortable. I once knew a woman who wore what she called "red hot green" stockings with a bright red-orange dress—but she was rail-slim and the epitome of self-confidence, and could get away with it.

Hats are far from being the ubiquitous accessory they once were—many women don't own even one—but a hat can give you a very "finished" look on special occasions, as well as serve a functional purpose (keep off sun or rain, protect you from cold) and still be attractive.

The short woman should avoid hats with large brims; but a hat with a crown that rises one or two inches above the top of the head will make her look taller.

Like shoes, a hat must fit perfectly—and it must flatter your head shape and size and your hairstyle. If your head is large, don't wear a big hat; if it's small, or if you're tall, don't wear a tiny one. The short woman should avoid hats with large brims or overly tall hats; but a hat with a crown that rises one or two inches above the top of the head will make her look taller. As a general rule, the big woman should wear medium-size hats that balance her figure.

If your neck isn't very short or overly thick, a colorful **scarf** can really give your outfit a sparkle. Scarves draw attention to the face, "light up" the colors of your clothes or your eyes, create vertical lines, tie together

Two ways to create the Thin Line with scarves.

the different parts of an outfit, and just look terrific. If you're not used to experimenting with scarves, this is the time to see what they can do for you. Don't buy cheap ones—they usually look cheap. Go to the scarf department of a good store; ask the saleswoman to show you some of the different ways they can be tied. You'll see so many beautiful scarves, in silk and cotton, you'll probably want to buy them all; but start with a couple that will work with several outfits.

In an earlier chapter we talked about some ways of using scarves. There are two basic things scarves can do to aid and abet the Thin Line: create height (little ones tied around your neck, above your collar or worn tucked into your collar) and create vertical lines (longer scarves, of silk so they'll drape and hang well, with the ends hanging to the waist or even lower). There are many variations of these two basic forms— go ahead and experiment. Just remember not to let a scarf create a *horizontal* line (by tying a short cotton scarf so the ends stick out towards your shoulders) and you won't go wrong. And in addition to regular square or oblong scarves, there are huge stoles and little string ties and ribbons of all sorts—all creating almost infinite variety.

Dresses or tops with self-fabric scarves or ties that hang down in front have a built-in thinner, and many garments are made this way these days. You can tie a floppy bow or a loose knot, high or low, or if it's one of the currently popular collarless styles with a little skinny string tie at the neck, just let it hang loose, with the throat gracefully exposed. You can let the ends of a long scarf hang loose over a jacket or blazer (tuck it under the collar in back). You can tie a scarf around your waist and create a vertical line from waist almost to hem. Tie it inside or outside the collar of your dress or blouse; replace a blouse under a suit with a scarf (a very sexy look!). You can really have fun with scarves...

...And with **jewelry.** Like scarves, jewelry can give dash and flair to what you're wearing, and can make you look more, or less, "dressed up." Jewelry can make you look like a million dollars—or feel like two cents. Remember that jewels are different from jewelry. Jewels are gems—diamonds, emeralds, garnets, and so on; while jewelry means any decorative ornament, whether made of precious stones, metal, bone, wood, shells, beads, leather, or whatever. The rule for jewelry is different from that for fabrics: the best polyester is that which most successfully counterfeits silk, linen or cotton, but the best jewelry is that which is proudly itself. Sooner wear a necklace of painted coffee beans than of rhinestones that are trying to look like diamonds.

Chokers are okay if you have a long neck; otherwise stick to long beads, chains or pendants.

Just as in clothes and shoes, simple, clean lines are the most attractive. Unless you're wearing a real Italian mosaic pendant, or a piece of antique gold with a complex and intricate design—in short, something made by an artist—let the material itself, its colors, shape and textures, create the effect.

The large woman shouldn't wear short necklaces. Chokers are okay if you have a reasonably long neck; otherwise, stick to long beads, chains or pendants in necklaces. If you have heavy arms, wear wide bracelets or a group of thin ones, rather than one delicate one alone. If you're large-busted, don't wear anything that draws attention to it, like large pendants. Chubby fingers? You can wear rings, but make sure they're not too tight—and wear wider ones or two or three skinny ones together.

Jewelry is the most erotic of adornments, and always has been. You've probably seen those ads for Monet costume jewelry—"in the golden manner of Monet." They take full advantage of jewelry's erotic potential. You can exploit this potential to your advantage by creating your own individual kind of eroticism. What are your best features? Delicate wrists? Wear a really beautiful bracelet that will emphasize them. Lovely hands? Wear two or three (no more!) exquisite rings. Try an ankle bracelet if you've nice ankles. Or if you have a smooth chest, wear a delicate chain or unusual necklace with a low-cut dress. Earrings play up the face, and a big woman can wear any kind to advantage except large round ones (on-the-ear or loop). Small, simple earrings are best unless you happen to have a pair of really gorgeous and unusual earrings that you want to be the focal point of your appearance (if so, keep your clothes very simple). As a rule, don't match earrings to your outfit or wear bright colors on your ears. Stick to gold, silver, pearl or semi-precious stones (small ones, please) such as jade, garnet or turquoise.

Caution: jewelry can very easily be overdone. If you're wearing earrings and bracelet, skip the necklace. Wearing a silver-and-turquoise pin on your black dress? Skip all other jewelry. Nothing is sillier than a woman who jangles and clanks because she's wearing seven pieces of jewelry at the same time.

Glasses. If you have to wear them—and more than half of all adults in our country do—you might as well let them enhance your appearance rather than detract from it. With the right frame color and shape, you can look just as good in glasses as without them (and maybe better).

Your facial structure is the first thing to keep in mind when buying frames. Spend plenty of time trying them on in front of a mirror. Avoid very large or very small frames or anything outlandish; like your accessories, glasses should blend in with your total appearance and not draw attention away from the rest of you. As a rule, they shouldn't hide your eyebrows or sit too high on the bridge of your nose, and the outsides of the frames shouldn't extend beyond the widest part of the cheekbone when seen from the front. If possible, take someone with you when you're trying on frames. Another person is usually a better judge of what is flattering to your face than you are yourself. Don't buy decorated frames; plain ones are best.

As for the color, it should be a quiet, preferably a neutral, tone, so it won't clash with anything you wear. If you have dark hair, you can wear black or brown, silver or gold frames; if your hair is light, try light brown, bone, beige, silver or gold. If you wear sunglasses, brown and gray are the best glass colors for the eyes and they'll go with anything.

Belts: you *can* wear them, but *not* the wide ones. For the large woman, the narrower the belt, the better. And of course it must never be tight. The best ones are self-belts or belts that are close to the color of the garment. Don't wear contrasting belts—they'll chop you right in half and destroy that nice l-o-n-g line you're trying to achieve. Keep the ends of self-tie belts long. The lines they form by falling vertically on a garment are slimming ones. If you want to tie a self-tie belt in a bow, make it a big, floppy one that hangs down, making a vertical line. But the slimming-est way to tie the best is in a plain knot with long strings.

5

SPORTSWEAR

The big woman needn't be afraid of active sports because she thinks she doesn't look good in sports clothing. Even bathing suits lose their terrors when you choose the right lines, fabrics and colors. With a little know-how, a big body can be the sexiest thing on the beach, the tennis courts, ski slopes, track or wherever the action is.

For the beach, stick to a one-piece suit unless you don't have an ounce of flab around the middle. There are more varieties of one-piecers today than ever before, though, so you're not consigning yourself to monotony. And don't feel that you must wear the old-fashioned, heavily constructed kind of bathing suit. The new lightweight suits without built-in bras or other artificial supports *can* be flattering and slimming—a little ingenious draping or seaming, which these suits frequently offer, can cover a multitude of pounds. Look for clean, simple vertical lines, no fussiness or shiny fabrics. You certainly don't have to stick to basic darks—wear the colors and patterns that please you—but avoid horizontal patterns.

If you feel you must have more "construction," make sure you buy a good suit that really fits *you*. Some bathing suits have absolutely rigid bras that make you

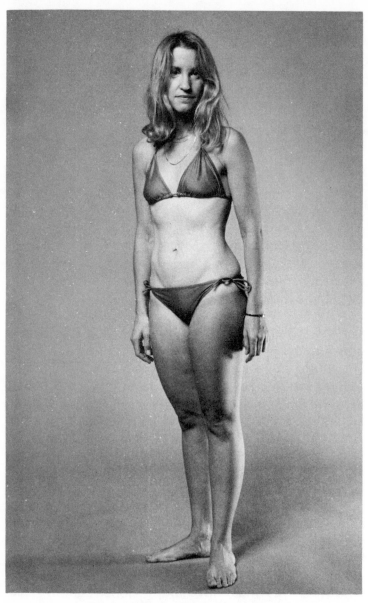

String bikinis are only for stringbeans.

Stick to a one-piece suit—a little ingenious draping or seaming can cover unwanted pounds.

The new light-weight suits without built-in bras or other artificial supports can be flattering and slimming.

look like you're in full armor. In general, avoid those oh-so-cute skirted suits unless you have really bulge-y thighs.

A word about Danskins: They were the first to come out with the sleek, lightweight bathing suits and they still make the best ones, in the largest variety of styles. There are lots of imitators, so look at the label. Clothing store personnel say Danskins are their best sellers in lightweight swimwear, as well as dancewear and other sportswear: they're well-made and wear well, they don't shrink or fade or lose their shape. Most of the competing brands just don't measure up.

There are lots of possibilities in beach cover-ups, too. Traditional cotton terrycloth can create unwanted bulk, but the new versatile stretch terries, usually made out of cotton-synthetic blends, can make for slenderizing beach wraps. The long, flowing lines of caftans are great for the large women, and they often have vertical or diagonal stripes, another plus. Beach wraps that match the bathing suit give you a well-put-together look that's always flattering. Just stay away from the short, boxy type of cover-up.

You'll find some of the most flattering sportswear around on the tennis courts, even if you've never thought you could wear one of those little white outfits (incidentally, they don't have to be white anymore). Most tennis outfits have clean, geometric lines and a minimum of detail—all to your advantage. The princess-style dress is tops. And who said you can't wear shorts? Just make sure they're not tight around the thighs and fit well at the waist.

Being comfortable and looking great on the ski slopes, the jogging trail, and the golf course is easier than you

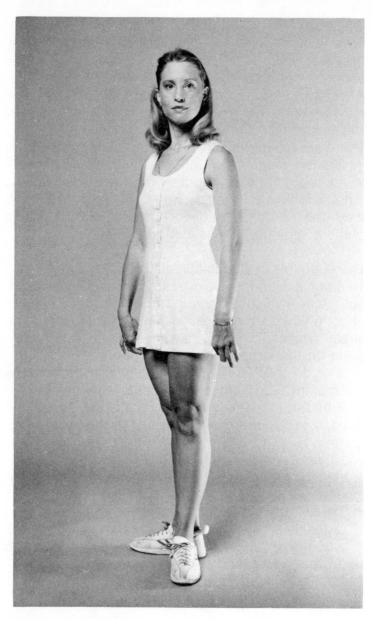

The princess-style tennis dress is tops.

Who said you can't wear shorts?

Reject those popular abominable-snowman-size down jackets in favor of something that hugs the body more closely.

think. Those ostensibly clingy ski pants are really a boon to the big woman, because the stirrups under the feet provide vertical stretch. Choose your jacket carefully, though. Bulk is not for you. Reject those popular abominable-snowman-size down jackets in favor of something that hugs the body more closely. Jogging clothes can be beautifully slimming, but please, no sweatshirts, shapeless T-shirts or drawstring-tied pants! Tailored jogging outfits, particularly the ones with vertical stripes down the sides, look elegant even when you're in a sweat. As for golf attire, its simplicity almost ensures good looks on the green. You can wear golf skirts, culottes, Bermuda shorts, slacks, with a tailored blouse or cotton knit top (remember, sportswear has to be comfortable and absorbent; cotton's your best bet).

6

DRESSING UP

Big women are *made* for dramatic evening clothes, and there's an almost inexhaustible variety to choose from these days, from long, soft, romantic dresses to dressy-but-casual disco wear. The drama in your evening clothes should be in the cut of the garments, the fabric, texture, color and pattern (if any)—nothing else. No billowing sleeves, bows, flounces or other unneeded extras to detract from the simple elegance of your outfit. Good bosom? Plunge as far as you feel comfortable, but make it a deep, not a wide neckline. Choose soft fabrics that drape well—chiffon (or simulate with good rayon), crepe de chine, silk jersey. No taffetas or satins except for contrasting trim or accents. You can wear prints for evening, either geometrics or florals, but step back and look at the pattern from a distance to make sure it doesn't give the impression of horizontal lines.

Don't clutter your evening look with a lot of jewelry. A pair of dramatic earrings and an attractive dinner ring should do the trick.

Casual dressing up is becoming more and more common, especially with the disco revolution. What do you wear to a party where cocktail clothes are too much and office wear will make you look like the chaperone?

Make it a deep, not a wide neckline.

Unfortunately, most casual-dressy clothes are made for skinnies, so you'll have to use some imagination. Here's the occasion for a silk or crepe tunic (dress it up with a light-as-air scarf) and pants, or a side-slit skirt with a big, blousy, soft top (the combination of the slinky skirt with its vertical lines and the soft fullness of the blouse is a winner). And, of course, jeans—the terrific ones we talked about earlier. If they fit beautifully, they'll go with the dressiest blouse. Try a gorgeous silk shirt, open the front three buttons' worth, turn up the collar (or wear one of the many lovely collarless or mandarin-collared styles), and put a narrow belt through the jeans.

If you're going to wear evening clothes, you have to have an evening wrap. Nothing is more fatmaking than inappropriate garb—a short trenchcoat over a full-length gown, for example. If you can afford an eve-

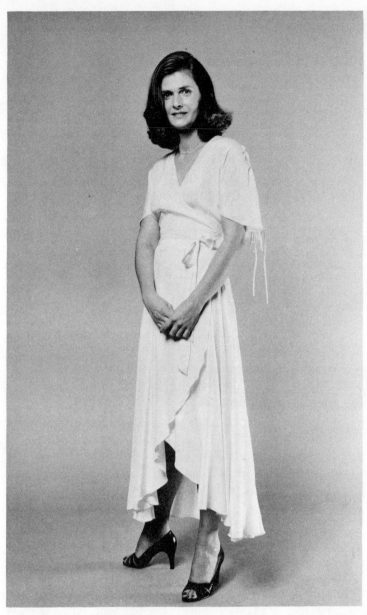

Choose soft fabrics that drape well.

The combination of a slinky skirt with its vertical lines and the soft full-ness of a blouse is a winner.

116

Nothing is more fatmaking than a short trenchcoat over a full-length gown.

117

ning coat, make it ankle-length or longer, in a neutral color. Keep it very simple and in a matte fabric: avoid satin, peau-de-soie, or any fabric that will make you look like a gleaming Mount Everest. If you don't have an evening coat, a knitted wrap will look just as pretty. A loosely crocheted triangle with fringe (you can make it yourself) will add a slenderizing V-line to your back as well as verticals in front. Finely-woven wool or mohair will add a soft, feminine look. And nothing makes a prettier summer evening wrap than a jumbo-sized silk scarf.

7

MAKEUP, HAIR, MOVEMENT

Up to now we've been talking about the body and the things you put on it. Now we're going to get to the part of you that people usually react to first—the part above the neck—and how it can add to the illusion of a slenderer you. By this point you should be pretty adept at disguising little body flaws; but whatever can't be completely disguised will actually seem to vanish if people's eyes are drawn to a pretty, perfectly made-up face, a beautifully coiffed head and a general impression of poise and grace.

Contrary to what a lot of women think, you don't need a "big" hairdo and a face burdened by a half inch of makeup for the head to attract attention. Oh, an outlandish hairstyle and inch-long eyelashes will get attention, all right—but it'll be the kind of attention that makes people shake their heads and say, "Who's she trying to be, Bozo the Clown?" Makeup is meant to enhance the face, not hide it. Less is more. The real trick is in knowing exactly how and where to put makeup.

Match your foundation to your skin tone and put it on *lightly*. Blend it carefully so there's no abrupt line at the hairline or under the jaw. A pinkish-beige or pinkish-peach blusher is good for most women—not too orange, not too rosy. Apply it on the cheekbones and blend up toward the temples. If your face is too wide or chubby, a bit of blusher down the sides of the cheeks, closest to the ears, will narrow it; and a dab under the chin, blended in well, will help camouflage a bit of a double chin. But remember to use a very light touch!

Next, the eyes, the focal point of your face. Curl the upper lashes with a dime-store eyelash curler (yes, they do work). Comb eyebrow hairs upward and pluck any stray hairs (but only stray ones—don't pluck any hairs out of the brow itself). Blend cake eye shadow in a soft color—gray, brown, gray-brown or gray-blue—over the outer half of the upper eyelid; then blend a little of it over the inner half, just enough to avoid a line of demarcation (these soft colors will make too-prominent eyes recede, too). For special occasions, you can blend the neutral color with a pastel—blue, green or lavender—to highlight the eyes even more. With a soft brown pencil, draw a thin line along the base of the upper lashes and smudge it a bit. Then two thin coats (never one thick one) of mascara—brown or dark gray, not black—and your eyes are dazzling.

The fashion moguls are trying to get us back to those bright red lipsticks of the '40's. Don't fall for it! Brightly painted lips are neither sensuous nor kissable. You certainly needn't go back to the colorless or nearly-white lips of a few years ago (in fact, the whitish tones are rather ghastly), but stick to soft colors—rose, peach, melon, salmon, etc. And don't go outside the natural outline of your lips—it never looks attractive.

(A note about nails: the dark colors always look like Dragon Lady. Use colorless if you have beautiful nails;

light pink or peach shades if they need a bit of help. And keep them medium length—extending just a fraction of an inch beyond the fingertips—and perfectly trimmed.)

If you feel you need help with makeup, there's usually someone in the cosmetics department of good stores who will show you how to make up perfectly. It will make her happy if you buy a makeup item from her, but it can be something inexpensive.

Your hair must be as right for you as your makeup to give your head that "finished" look that radiates elegance. The huge head is passe—even the Afro hairdo is smaller these days. Your hairstyle should be suited to your facial structure and type of hair; it should be simple and easy-to-care-for. Elaborate, "frozen" hairdos have been out for years, but lots of women haven't gotten the message yet.

Your hair shouldn't be cut or styled in any way that's unnatural for it; the way to really beautiful hair is to help it to follow its own growth pattern in the way that's most flattering to you. Curly, wavy and straight hair all have their own kind of beauty. Start with an expert cut—go to a hairdresser who has a good reputation and whose work you've admired. Tell him or her what you'd like but listen to his or her suggestions, too. And never mind what's currently the rage. Your hair has to look great on *you*, not on some model in a magazine.

To analyze the shape of your face, pull all of your hair back and look in the mirror. Not everyone has an oval face: many faces are basically square, round, oblong, triangular or heart-shaped. For the narrow-chinned face (the heart and triangle), a bit of fullness at chin

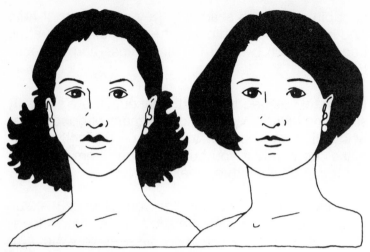

For the narrow-chinned face, a bit of fullness at the chin level is very becoming; if your jaw is very broad, less fullness at the jaw and more at ear level and above is what you want.

level is very becoming; if your jaw is very broad or the bottom of your face is round, less fullness at the jaw and more at ear level and above is what you want. For square and oblong faces, soft curls, in either a short or long length. Height at the top of the head (but not too much) elongates a face that's too round. The perfect oval shape (lucky you!) can wear almost any style well. Stick to soft lines and avoid harsh geometrics. Hair that gently frames the face is much more flattering than hair that's pulled severely back from it. And don't worry too much about length. Wear the length you like and feel comfortable with; length of hair is not a matter of age or station in life but of hair type, facial structure and personal taste.

Before we wind things up, let's talk for a minute about how you're going to carry this lovely new woman you've become. As though she's held together by Scotch tape and the slightest misstep might break

For square and oblong faces, soft curls are best.

her to pieces? Of course not. As though she's heavy and cumbersome? No way! You're going to carry yourself as though you were born willowy and are perfectly comfortable with the 120 lbs. you now look as though you weigh. No anxious checking of your appearance every time you pass a mirror. No nervous feeling around for possible bulges. No slumping, slouching, hunching, bunching, tensing or clunking around. No plopping into chairs. Stand in front of the mirror in one of your newly-put-together outfits and adopt various positions. See which are the most graceful and natural; then make them habitual. Adopt the "model's stance" —one foot pointing forward, the other slightly outward. Learn to keep your shoulders back and tummy in. When you sit, place one foot behind the other and gracefully lower yourself into the chair. Don't sit with knees apart or with one foot resting on the other knee. *Feel* like a beautiful woman and you will *move* like one. Feel and move like a slim, sensual, elegant and sexy woman, and you'll *be* one.

CONCLUSION

Anybody can be thin. All it takes is a good diet book and an honest obsession with torturing your body into unnaturally tiny proportions. For a normal woman of normal appetites, dressing thin means looking great, no matter what your size. Anyone can do it, using a combination of 1/10 optical illusion and 9/10 attitude. The result is a new you: a woman who enjoys and appreciates herself and knows she's beautiful.

Don't, Don't, Don't!

Don't allow shop clerks to bulldoze you. *You* know what you like, you know when you look good. Saleswomen tend to tell you an outfit's "stunning" even if it makes you look like Moby Dick. Use your own eyes.

Don't buy something because your friend likes it, your daughter owns it, or you see it in magazines.

Don't constantly wear overblouses and other camouflaging garments that make you look like a walking, talking tepee.

Don't dress 20 years older than you are. Big is not old.

Don't dress like you're in mourning. Big girls look as smashing in dusty rose, teal blue or subdued prints as skinnies.

Don't pretend to be invisible. Unless you're a professional spy, it's unlikely that you *really* slip unnoticed through the shadows. Carry yourself proudly!

Do, Do, Do!

Do take good care of your clothing. Keep everything you own in top condition, so you never have to pass up the thing you want to wear—whether it's a blouse, scarf, shoes, jewelry, whatever—because it's dirty or torn or needs hemming or pressing or repairing.

Do keep your closet and drawers organized, so you know what you have and can always find the perfect item.

Do dress in front of the mirror (full-length, please) each morning, and check for imperfections. Bunching under the arm? A new bra or a different top is in order. Horizontal creases across the lap? Save that skirt for ironing! Once you're satisfied that your appearance is perfect, forget it.

Do look great *all* the time, even if you're just going around the corner for a loaf of bread.

Do be proud of your good points. Shapely bosom? Flaunt it! Lovely hands? Play them up with pretty cuffs, a gorgeous bracelet or ring, perfectly manicured fingernails.

The world is full of healthy, good-looking women who have flesh in abundance. Nobody can accuse Dolly

Parton of starving herself for her art, nor is radiant Beverly Sills a cadaver. They're big and beautiful and they like themselves. And there's every reason in the world for you to like yourself, too. When you like yourself, you feel great...when you feel great, you're beautiful.

The models who appear in this book are

GUN DRONGE   **JOANNA WEBER**

Photography by Stuart Miller